FOOD ENZYMES
The Missing Link to Radiant Health

FOOD ENZYMES
The Missing Link to Radiant Health

Humbart Santillo B.S., M.H.

Edited by Deborah Kantor

HOHM PRESS

Hohm Press, Box 2501, Prescott, Arizona 86302

First Edition published 1987, Second printing 1991.
Printed in the United States of America

Library of Congress Cataloging in Publication Data

Santillo, Humbart
        Food Enzymes: The Key To Radiant Health

        Bibliography: p.
        Includes index.
        1. Enzymes—Therapeutic use.   2. Nutrition.
        3. Health.   I. Title.
RM666.E55S26   1987   612'.39   87-8707
ISBN 0-934252-11-4 (pbk.)

The theories and formulas presented in this book are expressed as the author's opinion and as such are not meant to be used to diagnose, prescribe, or to administer in any manner to any physical ailments. In any matters related to your health please contact a qualified, licensed health practitioner.

DEDICATION

To: Tony Collier, National Enzyme Company and
      Lou Piccone, N.F.L. Alumnist

When a man needs answers he must reach out and seek
from those who are closest to him. These men provided
me with that avenue. Thank you.

TABLE OF CONTENTS

Introduction 1

What a food enzyme is 2

What do food enzymes do in the body?..................... 3

How do food enzymes get their names?..................... 4

Where do we get our food enzymes?......................... 6

How food enzymes aid digestion 11

Food enzymes and longevity................................ 14

Food enzymes and their relationship to disease 19

The endocrine system and food enzymes 23

Obesity and circulatory diseases........................... 25

Raw food diet and predigestion 31

Body, mind and food enzymes 36

Detoxification and food enzymes........................... 40

Children and food enzymes 49

The use of food enzymes in
          the prevention of allergies and candida.............. 53

Sports—food enzymes—and nutrition 56

Who should take food enzymes?............................ 59

Reference and food enzymes bibliography 62

INTRODUCTION

Throughout my years of experience as a health practitioner, author, and researcher I have developed a certain understanding, and that is — there is no singular formula, food or health product that is a "cure-all." Even though I intellectually felt this to be true, I firmly believed that there was something that every person could use during therapy, or as a health supplement, that could act as foundation and adjunct to both medical and non-medical therapies. Now I feel my wish has come true! I found that food enzymes were what I have been searching for. If you are interested in longevity, vitality, superior health, overcoming sickness, or if you are having trouble losing weight, and feel that after taking vitamins and minerals for years, you haven't really benefited as much as you would like to, this book should be of interest to you.

Three years ago, Viktoras Kulvinskas, author of *"Survival into the 21st Century"*, sent me a book written by Dr. Edward Howell, called *"Food Enzymes for Health and Longevity."* This book explained to me why some therapies work and why some don't — because of enzymes. Enzymes are needed for every chemical action and reaction in the body. Our organs, tissues, and cells are all run by metabolic enzymes. Minerals, vitamins, and hormones need enzymes to be present in order to do their work properly. Enzymes are the labor force of the body. In 1966, a Scottish medical journal stated, "Each of us, as with all living organisms, could be regarded as an orderly, integrated succession of enzyme reactions."

WHAT AN ENZYME IS

It has always been felt that enzymes are protein molecules. This is incorrect. Let me clarify this by giving you an example: a light bulb can only light up when you put an electric current through it. It is animated by electricity. The current is the life force of the bulb. Without electricity we would have no light, just a light bulb, a physical object without light. So, we can say that the light bulb actually has a dual nature: a physical structure, and a non-physical electrical force that expresses and manifests through the bulb. The same situation exists when trying to describe what an enzyme is within our body structure.

Let me try to define enzymes and a few properties about them. An *enzyme* is said to be a protein molecule and each acts in certain ways in the body doing specific jobs such as digesting food, building protein in the bones and skin and aiding detoxification, to name a few. Once we cook food at high temperatures though, the enzyme is destroyed. It no longer carries on its designated function. Although the physical protein molecule is still present, it has lost its life force. Much like a battery that has lost its power, the physical structure remains but the electrical energy which once animated it is no longer present. A protein molecule is actually only the carrier of enzyme activity. In experiments described in "*Chemical Reviews*" (1933), the activity of one protein molecule was transferred over to another protein substance, leaving the original molecule devoid of its original activity.[1] This only proves further that an enzyme is the invisible activity or energy factor and not just the protein molecule itself. So, for clarity, let us agree that a protein molecule is a carrier of the enzyme activity, much like the light bulb is the carrier for an electrical current.

WHAT DO ENZYMES DO IN THE BODY?

Enzymes are involved in every process of the body. Life could not exist without them. Enzymes digest all of our food and make it small enough to pass through the minute pores of the intestines into the blood. Enzymes in the blood take prepared, digested food and build it into muscles, nerves, blood and glands. They assist in storing sugar in the liver and muscles, and turn fat into fatty tissue. Enzymes aid in the formation of urea which is to be eliminated as urine and also in the elimination of carbon dioxide in the lungs. There is an enzyme that builds phosphorus into bone and nerve tissue, and another to help attach iron to red blood cells. Male sperm carries enzymes that dissolve the tiny crevice in the female egg membrane, so it may gain entrance into it. An enzyme called streptokinase is used in medicine to dissolve blood clots. Enzymes in our immunity system attack waste materials and poisons in the blood and tissues. These few examples exemplify the importance of enzymes to our everyday body functions, Howell IX.[2]

The number of enzymes in the body is overwhelming, and yet each one has a specific function. A protein digestive enzyme will not digest a fat, a fat digestive enzyme will not digest a starch. This is frequently called enzyme specificity. Let us say: they are very intelligent when it comes to their activity and functions. Enzymes act upon substance and change them into another substance, either chemical, or a type of by-product, but remain unchanged themselves. Any substance that an enzyme acts upon is called a substrate. The substrate is then changed from its original identity by the enzyme to another substance with a different identity. Each enzyme is believed to fit into a specific geometrical design as shown in Diagram 1. Enzymes do a tremendous amount of work.

DIAGRAM 1

HOW AN ENZYME WORKS

ENZYME BEFORE WORKING   MOLECULE COMPLETE

ENZYME WHILE WORKING

ENZYME AFTER WORKING   MOLECULE SPLIT
                                    APART

From *The Chemicals of Life*
by Isaac Asimov
Illustration by John Bradford
Published by New American Library
New York and Scarsborough, Ontario 1954

HOW DO ENZYMES GET THEIR NAMES?

Due to the volume of enzymes, there had to be a system of nomenclature which was devised by the National Enzyme Commision. We now know that the names of all enzymes end in "-ase," and in most cases, the name of the enzyme will also reveal its function; thus, protease is an enzyme that catalyzes (acts upon) proteins, lipase is an enzyme which catalyzes fats, cellulase is an enzyme which acts upon cellulose, and amylase acts upon starches.[3]

There are four categories of food enzymes. They are:

1. Lipase - which serves to break down fat
2. Protease (proteolytic enzymes) - works to break down protein
3. Cellulase - assists in breaking down cellulose
4. Amylase - which breaks down starch

Included in each category are a number of enzymes. For example, trypsin and pepsin act upon proteins, so they are proteolytic enzymes which fall under the category of protease. (The word proteolytic is just the singular form of the word protease.) Trypsin and pepsin do not end in "-ase" because they were named before the new nomenclature came into being. However, even these enzymes have been called trypsinogenase and pepsinogenase. Do not let the verbiage confuse you or cause you to lose interest in enzymes. The names are not important unless you are going to make enzymes a study. What is important is that you understand how to get enzymes into your body, their sources, and that without them life cannot exist. As we become enzyme deficient, the faster we age. The more we store up our enzyme reserve, the healthier we will be. We will learn how to increase our enzyme reserve later in this book.

WHERE DO WE GET OUR ENZYMES?

We usually think of enzymes as involved only in digesting our food so we can absorb it. Very seldom do we find informative material that demonstrates that enzymes are involved in every metabolic process. Our immunity system, bloodstream, liver, kidneys, spleen, pancreas, as well as our ability to see, think, and breathe depend upon enzymes. The lack of them in any of these areas can prove to be detrimental in degrees of depletion. Realizing that the lack of enzymes can be a predisposing cause of disease substantiates their importance. There is much literature which tries to establish that toxicity and genetics are the predisposing cause of disease. These are true statements, but the important thing to keep in mind is that all cellular activity is initiated by enzymes. Enzymes break down toxic substances so that the body can eliminate them without damaging the eliminative organs.

It is important that we preserve the body's enzyme level at all expenses. There are two ways to preserve and replenish our enzyme level: by eating raw food and by taking enzyme supplements. Supplementing enzymes to our diet and eating a raw food diet are subjects that will be discussed throughout this book. What is important at this time is to understand what happens when we cook our food. The difference between live (raw) and dead food is enzymatic activity. If you had two seeds and boiled one, which one would grow when placed in soil? There is no question that the unboiled seed would sprout because it has its enzymes intact. All foods provided by nature have an abundance of enzymes when in their raw state.

One characteristic of enzymes is their inability to withstand hot temperatures such as those used in cooking. Consequently, the enzymes are completely destroyed in all foods that are canned, pasteurized, baked, roasted, stewed or fried. At 129°F all enzymes are destroyed. Baking bread kills enzymes. Most butters have no enzymes because they are pasteurized. Canned juices may have vitamins and minerals, but the heating process has killed the enzymes. The roasted breakfast cereals that we feed our children, are devoid of enzymes. When live food substances come in contact with heated water, the enzymes are destroyed quite rapidly. Dr. Howell in his book on food enzymes states, "Enzymes are more or less completely destroyed when heated in water in the temperature range between 48° to 65°C. Long heating at 48°C or short heating at 65°C, kills enzymes. Heating at 60° to 80°C for one-half hour completely kills any enzymes."[4]

Food processing, refining, cooking, and more recently the advent of micro-waving are detrimental processes that are causing dramatic changes in the food that we eat. They have rendered our foods enzyme-deficient, causing imbalances in our organs, acting as a predisposing cause of disease. Enzymes are always a part of animal and plant life. They are a component part of living matter. Animals in the wild consume large amounts of enzymes as a result of their primary raw food diets. This aids in the digestive process, taking the stress off organs such as the pancreas, liver, and spleen which would otherwise have to produce large amounts of enzymes. This causes unwarranted stress on these organs and body tissues decreasing the longevity of the body.

There are three major classes of enzymes: metabolic enzymes (enzymes which work in blood, tissues, and organs), food enzymes from raw food, and digestive enzymes. Our organs are run by metabolic enzymes. These enzymes take food substances and build them into healthy tissue and have numerous other duties. One authority found ninety-eight enzymes working in the arteries alone. Since 1968, thirteen hundred enzymes have been identified. A shortage of these enzymes may cause serious health problems.

Nature has placed enzymes in food to aid in the digestive process instead of forcing the body's enzymes to do all of the work. It is to be remembered that we inherited an enzyme reserve at birth and this quantity can be decreased as we age by eating an enzyme-deficient diet. By eating most of our food cooked, our digestive systems have to produce all of the enzymes, thus causing an enlargement of the digestive organs. To supply supply such enzymes, the body draws on its reserve from all organs and tissues, causing a metabolic deficit. If each of us would take in more exogenous enzymes (those enzymes taken from outside sources), our enzyme reserve would not be depleted at such a rapid pace. This would keep our metabolic enzymes more evenly distributed throughout the organism. This is one of the most health-promoting measures that one could implement into his or her daily lifestyle.

The pancreas, which is of primary importance to our digestive system, secretes lipase (fat digestive enzymes), amylase (starch digestive enzymes), and protease (protein digestive enzymes). The question is: Does this organ produce all of these enzymes from within itself? At the University of Toronto, the pancreases from sixteen dogs were removed. These dogs were kept alive for months by the use of insulin and were shown to have normal levels of amylase in their blood streams.[5] The School of Medicine at Yale University, doing a similar study, found that six dogs had a rise in blood amylase amounting to twenty times the normal amount after the ligation (tying off) of the pancreatic duct.[6] In a 1936 "Journal of Enzymology," Fiessinger and Associates could not find a significant change in the lipase content of the blood of dogs fifteen days following the removal of their pancreases. The enzymes that maintain blood levels after the pancreas is removed come from other tissues and organs.[7] [8] It is foolish to believe that an organ weighing just a few ounces (the average pancreas weighs only 85 grams) can supply the enormous amount of enzymes needed in the body day after day, year after year. It can be substantiated that the pancreas receives constituents (enzymes) from the blood and tissues. Dr. Willstatter has demonstrated the presence of amylase in white blood cells (leucocytes) and also shown that the white blood cells have proteolytic enzymes similar to the secretions of the pancreas.[9] White blood cells have a greater variety of enzymes than does the pancreas. Leukocytes travel through the body, destroying foreign substances in the bloodstream, working as part of the immune system, protecting us against disease. We lose enyzmes daily through our sweat, urine, feces, and through all digestive fluids including salivary and intestinal secretions. Logic dictates that a pancreas weighing only a few ounces could not possibly be responsible for the production of all of the enzymes found throughout the body of a 150-pound man. Enzymes are found in every tissue of the body. Even when the pancreas is removed, the body still maintains a certain enzyme level.

Another point of paramount importance is that a percentage of enzymes which are taken orally, or the ones already present in raw food, can be absorbed in the intestines and utilized in the body's metabolic processes helping prevent enzyme depletion. Before we look at the absorption of enzymes, let's look at other substances that are absorbed through the intestines.

At the University of Illinois, compressed yeast fed to dogs produced positive yeast cultures in the liver, lymph glands, lungs, spleen, and kidneys, proving that whole yeast cells were absorbed.[10] Dr. Oelgoetz documented in the American Journal of Digestion that if patients with low levels of blood amylase are given an extract of whole pancreas which contains amylase, the normal blood level can be restored within one hour and remain normal for days after administration.[11]

It is a well-known fact that unassimilated proteins, yeast cells, carbohydrates and fats can be reabsorbed into the blood stream, causing allergies, skin diseases, and other illnesses.[12] Dr. Oelgoetz proved that when pancreatic enzymes are administered to patients having allergies accompanied by low blood levels of enzymes, this level returns to normal and the allergy subsides. Functional digestive disturbances, hyperacidity, and skin problems were relieved the same way. Clinicians have effectively relieved a variety of skin diseases caused by incompletely digested food materials. The blood provides the ideal environment for enzymes to cause a partial breakdown of undigested materials.

The oral administration of proteolytic enzymes for inflammation and sports injuries have been used for years by Max Wolf, M.D. and Karl Ransberger, Ph.D. In one experiment in their book, "Enzymes Therapy," certain enzymes were tagged with a radioactive dye to see if these enzymes could be followed through the digestive tract into the bloodstream. It was shown through electrophoretic investigations that the radioactive dye tagged to the enzymes, could be found in the liver, spleen, kidneys, heart, lungs, duodenum and urine.[13]

If you would like more information showing how enzymes, taken orally, are absorbed and used throughout the body taking the stress off other enzyme-producing organs, see the references in the back of this book. For now, let's take a look at how the enzymes function in raw food and how they may aid in the digestive process, preparing bodily functions.

HOW FOOD ENZYMES AID DIGESTION

A human being is not maintained by his food intake, but rather, by what is digested. Every food must be broken down by enzymes to simpler building blocks. Enzymes may be divided into two groups: exogenous (found in raw food), and endogenous (produced within our bodies). The more one gets of the exogenous enzymes, the less will have to be borrowed from other metabolic processes and supplied by the pancreas. The enzymes contained in raw food actually aid in the digestion of that same food when it is chewed. One can live for many years on a cooked food diet but eventually this will cause cellular enzyme exhaustion which lays the foundation for a weak immunity system and ultimately disease. Dr. Howell states, "Researchers show that cooked food with the fiber broken down passes through the digestive system more slowly than raw foods. Partially it ferments, rots, putrifies, throwing back into the body toxins, gas, and causing heartburn and degenerative diseases."

It is important to realize that the enzymes in raw food actually digest 5 to 75 percent of the food itself *without* the help of the enzymes secreted by the body. This is called energy conservation since the body does not have to supply 100% of the enzymes to digest the food. At the Institute of Animal Physiology, Agriculture College, Berlin, comparative experiments were done to show that the enzymes contained in raw food aid digestion. Fowl do not have amylase (starch digestive enzyme) in their salivary secretions. In one study, chickens were fed ground barley which has a good amount of pure starch in it. After five hours, the stomach contents of the fowl were analyzed showing that eight percent of the starch was digested.[14] It was also demonstrated by Dr. Boas, as reported by Dr. Howell, "the enzymes in bananas were activated in the intestines to aid in the digestive process."[15] This also shows that not all enzymes are destroyed in the stomach, but merely inactivated there and then reactivated again in the intestines. This important point was also proven by Russian researcher, Dr. Matveev. He demonstrated that oxidase and catalase, which are enzymes supplied from carrot juice, were inactivated in the stomach because of the acidity, and then reactivated again in the alkalinity of the small intestines.[16] In summary, the enzymes in raw food digest a small percentage of the food. It appeared then that all enzymes are not destroyed in the stomach as once believed, but are actually reactivated again to aid the pancreas in digestion in the small intestine.

We all suffer the consequences of a cooked food diet. As Dr. Howell demonstrates, the pancreases of animals subsisting exclusively on raw plant food are much smaller relative to its body weight than human's.[17] The pancreas of a human weighing 140 pounds, weighs 85-90 grams; the pancreas of a sheep weighing 85 pounds, weighs only 18.8 grams; the pancreas of a 1005 pound cow, weighs only 308 grams; and the pancreas of a horse weighing 1200 pounds, weighs only 330 grams. Calculated as a percentage of body weight, the following figures are presented.

	Body Weight Grams	Pancreas Weight % of Body Weight
Sheep	38,505	0.0490
Cattle	455,265	0.0680
Horse	543,600	0.0603
Man	63,420	00.1400

Notice how little man weighs compared to cattle and horses, and again in comparison, how much larger his pancreas is. This is because the pancreas must enlarge because it is being overworked by consuming a cooked food diet devoid of enzymes. The fascinating point here is that in humans, the saliva contains amylase to aid the pancreas in starch digestion. Herbivora (animals listed in the chart) have relatively no amylase in their saliva, and their pancreases still remain their normal size without enlarging. The answer seems to be that the raw food of herbivora supplies active enzymes which participate in digestion taking stress off the digestive organs, the pancreas, and in fact, the whole body's metabolism.

A similar experiment was reported in the Phillipine Journal of Science (Vol. 52) as performed by the School of Hygiene of Public Health in 1933. The school performed 768 postmortum examinations of Phillipinos. The observations showed that the pancreases of the Phillipinos were twenty-five to fifty percent heavier than Europeans and Americans, because cooked rice was their staple food and was eaten as much as three times a day. This caused their pancreases to be overworked, secreting large amounts of enzymes, particularly amylase causing an enlargement of the organ. An enlarged organ is often a pathological condition, showing the beginning signs of degeneration.

It is a fact that a cooked food diet shows a larger outpouring of enzymes from our digestive organs. At first thought, it might be presumed that hypertrophied (enlarged) organs is a desirable accommodation, but it has always been shown that enlargement of an organ is accompanied by the excessive function of that organ, followed by exhaustion and degeneration. Since the enzymes in raw food actually help digest the food they are contained in, and can be absorbed into the blood and used in other metabolic processes, we can assume that taking enzymes or eating a large percentage of raw food, will help take the stress off not only the pancreas, but the entire body.

ENZYMES AND LONGEVITY

The comparative study of the enzyme content of the blood, urine, and digestive fluids of the human population can present some very important data. The average diet is predominately heat-treated and possesses only a fraction of its original enzyme content. It has been shown that young adults have a high value of enzyme reserve in their tissues. In older persons, the potential enzyme tissue reserve is much lower and essentially depleted. When a young person eats cooked food, there is a greater outpouring of enzymes from the organs and body fluids than in adults. This is because years of eating a cooked food diet has depleted the adult, whereas the young adult's tissue reserve is still at maximum.

A further experiment in relation to saliva and its amylase content was performed at the Michael Reese Hospital in Chicago. Used in the experiment were young adults from the ages of 21 to 31 and another group ranging from age 69 to 100. It was shown that the younger group had 30 times more amylase in their saliva than the elderly group. This is why younger persons can tolerate a diet of white bread, starches, and predominately cooked food. But as our enzyme reserve is depleted over the years, these same foods can cause illnesses such as constipation, blood diseases, bleeding ulcers, bloating, and arthritis. In older individuals, the enzyme content of the body has been depleted and these foods are not properly digested. They ferment in the digestive tract producing toxins that are then absorbed into the blood and deposited in the joints and other soft-tissue areas.

A chronic disease is a disease that has lingered in the body for many weeks or months and sometimes years. It has been a constant drag on the body, depleting it of its enzymes, vitamins, minerals, and trace minerals. During chronic diseases, there is usually a low body reserve of enzymes. In 111 Japanese patients who had tuberculosis, 82% of them had lower enzyme contents than normal individuals. As the disease worsened, the enzyme level decreased.[18] Dr. Volodin, in the Archives Vendanugskrankh, found after studying the enzyme level of urine, blood, and intestines, that it was usually decreased in diabetes. Studies of feces showed incomplete digestion of meat and fats in many cases. In five of six diabetic patients, the lipase and trypsin (proteolytic enzyme) of the pancreatiuc juice was found to be decreased.[19] Dr. Ottenstein in a similar study pattern showed low blood amylase levels in skin affections such as psoriasis, dermatitis, and pruritis.[20] Another interesting experiment showed that 40 patients suffering from liver diseases such as cirrhosis, hepatitis, and cholecystitis (inflammation of the gallbladder), showed low levels of amylase. It was found that when there was a rise in the blood amylase level, there was an improvement in the general condition of each patient, as well as an improvement in the liver condition.[21]

It is undisputable fact that during chronic disease we find a lower enzyme content in blood, urine, feces, and tissues. In acute diseases, and sometimes at the beginning of chronic diseases, the enzyme content is often found to be high. This shows that the body has a reserve, and the tissues are not yet depleted, consequently, there is a larger outpouring of enzymes in the battle against disease. As the disease progresses, the body's enzyme content is lowered.

This correlation, between a diminished enzyme content during chronic disease and old age, is something that is many times misunderstood. A low enzyme content in old age is often looked upon as "normal." A low content during chronic diseases is considered a pathological state. The truth of the matter is that age is not so much a matter of how many years one has been alive, but rather is a matter of the integrity of the tissues of the body. These tissues depend upon the amount of enzymes present to carry on the metabolism of every cell of the body. It is common to find a 60-year-old man or woman with a body of someone in his or her 40's.

There is a definite correlation between the amount of

enzymes an individual possesses and the amount of energy they have. Increasing age shows a slow decrease in enzyme reserve. When the enzyme level becomes so low that metabolism suffers, death will finally result. Any time the metabolism is falsely stimulated by coffee, a high protein diet, or other stimulants, the metabolism increases, enzymes are used up, a false energy output is experienced, and the individual feels a sense of well-being. The end result will be lower energy, a more rapid burn-out of enzymes, and premature old age. At Brown's University a group of 158 animals were over-fed and they lived on the average 29.6 days. Another group was maintained on a starvation diet, given only small amounts of food and fluid and they lived on the average 39.19 days — an increase of about 40%.[22] This study should at the very least make each of us look at our own intake and determine if we are indeed overingesting.

A high protein diet is very stimulating to the body and can cause serious damage. When the diet consists of more protein than is needed, the excess is broken down by enzymes in the liver and kidneys. The major by-product of protein breakdown is urea which is a diuretic. The kidneys are caused to urinate more fluid. Along with water, minerals are lost in the urine. One of the most important losses is calcium. Experiments have shown that when subjects consumed 75 grams of protein daily, even with an intake as high as 1400 milligrams of calcium, more calcium was lost in the urine than was actually absorbed.[23] This deficiency must be made up by the body's calcium reserve which is taken from the bones. Deficient bones are a stepping stone to osteoporosis (a condition when the bones break easily). The aforementioned experiments all show that when excessive amounts of protein, or food in general, are eaten, there is a corresponding decrease in enzyme, vitamin and mineral levels.

At the University of Toronto, a team of scientists showed that life runs its course in direct proportion to the catabolic rate. (The catabolic rate is the rapidity of the wear and tear of the body or the rate of tissue breakdown. This is in direct proportion to the aging process.) This tissue breakdown is performed by enzymes. The faster the breakdown, the more enzymes are used up. Our enzyme reserve can be used up rapidly or it can be preserved. Taking enzyme supplements and eating raw foods are ways to add enzymes to our enzyme reserve and add to our energy level.

Dr. Howell further states that, "Enzymes are a true yardstick of vitality. Enzymes offer an important means of calculating the vital energy of an organism. That which we call energy, vital force, nerve energy, and strength, may be synonomous with enzyme activity." Our logic tells us that the building up and the breaking down of tissues is performed by enzymes. In other words, our metabolism is maintained by enzyme activity. When our enzyme level is lowered, our metabolism is lowered, and so is our energy level. Do not misunderstand this statement. We are not saying that the source of life is enzymes, but that there is a correlation between enzyme levels and the youth of the tissues of an organism and energy levels.

Investigations have shown that in warm temperatures, enzymes are used up more rapidly than in cool temperatures. When starch-digesting enzymes are added to potato starch and placed in a room with a temperature of 80°F, the starch is digested much faster than starch with enzymes placed in a temperature of 40°F. As the temperature is increased, the enzymes work harder and are used up faster. The prevalent thought here is that enzymes are not actually used up, but many tests have shown that various enzymes are found in the urine after fevers and athletic activity. Enzymes are found in the urine, feces, and sweat, along with the used-up substances from proteins, enzymes, fats, carbohydrates, vitamins, and minerals.

Other food substances, such as vitamins and minerals, are replaced daily in our food intake. Not enough attention is placed on taking enzyme supplements or eating raw food. If we do not replenish our enzyme level and only consider vitamins and minerals, it is self-defeating. The body has to replace enzymes from within itself, stealing enzymes from all parts of the body, which in the end causes exhaustion, premature aging and a low energy system.

The utilization of vitamins depends upon enzymes and enzymes often depend on vitamins. Under clinical observation it has been shown that when taking vitamins combined in capsules with enzymes, smaller amounts of vitamins and minerals are needed. A good example of this was seen in a patient known personally by the author, who needed 70 milligrams of zinc daily to overcome a severe depletion. When zinc was combined with certain enzymes, this patient needed only 3 *micrograms* daily. This was drastic reduction. It seems that the body only needs small amounts of vitamins and minerals when combined with enzymes. Being good consumers, all of us are interested in saving money and this is possible by our needing smaller intakes of vitamins and minerals. Therefore, fewer capsules and tablets would be needed to maintain our daily requirements. It has been the experience of many clinicians that a patient is more likely to follow a health regimen if it can be made as easy and practical as possible.

ENZYMES AND THEIR RELATIONSHIP
TO DISEASE

Enzymes are a part of every metabolic process in the body — from the working of our glands to the proper functioning of our immune system. This is a general way of looking at the working of enzymes in our bodies. Specifically, from the individual disease standpoint, enzymes can be related, or at least discussed, in previous reference in their relationship to every disease.

When certain enzymes are in excess in the bloodstream, they can be used for diagnosing specific diseases. Lipase breaks down triglycerides into fatty acids and glycerol. The pancreas secretes a large amount of lipase (it draws much of the lipase from the blood) into the digestive tract. Where lipase is found in elevated levels in the blood, it can point specifically to a pancreatic disease. Serum lipase levels rise when pancreatic inflammation occurs. Acid phosphatase breaks down phosphates in the blood. These enzymes are found in the prostate gland, red blood cells, and platelets. There blood serum level activity is measured primarily to evaluate the presence of prostatic carcinoma (a malignant growth). Enzymes not only play a role in digestion, but also during disease and other metabolic processes.

The speed of the metabolism is determined by the activity of enzymes. The more rapidly the metabolism is working, the more enzymes are required to participate, and the faster the enzymes will be used up. During exercise and in acute diseases, the enzyme level can be found to be increased. Dr. Gerner, in a study done in 1933, made 300 amylase level determinations on 115 subjects, representing 28 different acute infectious diseases. The urinary amylase was increased in 73% of them. During pneumonia, acute appendicitis, malaria, pulmonary tuberculosis, fevers of all types, and children's diseases, enzymes were found to be elevated in blood, urine, and feces.[24] Any increase in metabolic activity, whether it is associated with fevers, heart action (exercise), digestion, muscular work, or pregnancy, is paralleled with an increase in enzyme activity. It is important to note that enzyme activity is increased as temperatures increase and is present in most acute disease conditions, fevers, and during exercise. In other words, enzymes perform more work during fevers of 104°F than at normal body temperatures. It is evident that if enzymes respond to fevers and infections, they have a direct relationship to the defense mechanism in our bodies. Keep in mind though that similarly when fevers decrease, so does the enzyme activity. This understanding of enzymes being used up more rapidly during disease, detoxification, digestion, in fact, every time our metabolism is speeded up, shows the importance of supporting our enzyme reserves at all times. It is true that during youth, the body can respond to such stimulation, but only to borrow against future enzyme resources.

There is a connection between the strength of our immune system and our enzyme level. The greater the amount of enzyme reserves, the stronger our immune system, the healthier and stronger we will be. It has been clearly stated that enzyme activity increases during digestion and also during any other increase in metabolism, such as acute diseases. But what is the exact correlation between our immune system and enzymes?

Our white blood cells (leukocytes) are responsible for destroying foreign disease-producing substances in the blood and lymph fluid in the body. During acute diseases and infections, the white blood cell count increases to help fight off these pathologies. Dr. Willstatter, in an early enzyme research study, demonstrated that there were 8 different amylase enzymes found in leukocytes.[25] Investigations also have shown that leukocytes contain proteolytic and lipolytic enzymes which are also common to those secreted by the pancreas. These enzymes act very much like the enzymes which are in our digestive tract (breaking down proteins, fats, and carbohydrates that have been absorbed by the blood causing diseased conditions.) [26] [27] Enzymes act as scavengers in the body. They latch onto foreign substances and reduce them to a form that the body can dispose of. They also prevent the arteries from clogging up and joints from becoming gummed up. It was always thought that the pancreas produced all of these enzymes, but as was mentioned earlier, this idea is erroneous. As small as the pancreas is, it couldn't possibly produce all of the enzymes found in the muscles, glands and tissues, plus produce those used up daily in digestion, and those lost in the sweat, urine, and feces. Enzymes are produced by all the tissues and cells of the body. And, in fact, it has been shown that the enzymes found in the white blood cells act very much like the enzymes found in the pancreas, expecially the proteolytic enzymes. Dr. Willstatter found it remarkable how closely the enzyme systems of white blood cells and the pancreatic gland agree with one another. Since the same enzymes are found in the white blood cells as are found in the pancreas, and since white blood cells transport these enzymes throughout the body, it seems that the pancreas and other enzyme-secreting glands receive a great portion of these enzymes via the leucocytes. After eating a cooked food meal, when digestive enzymes are desperately needed, the white blood cell count increases, seemingly to aid in the digestive process. Since every metabolic process is, at all times, interdependent and interrelated, this increase in the white blood cell count after the ingestion of a cooked meal, indicates a definite compensatory measure.

The body must supply a large amount of digestive enzymes because the enzymes that were once present in the food, were destroyed by the heating process. Dr. Kautchakoff, in his book demonstrating the relation of cooking and its effects on our systems, showed that there was an increase in white blood cells after eating a cooked food meal.[28] This increase in leukocytes is needed to transport enzymes to the digestive tract. He also showed that after a raw food meal, there was no substantial increase in leucocytes, showing that the body has to work much harder to produce and transport enzymes for digestion after a cooked food meal. It is important to remember that enzymes in raw food aid in the digestive process and this takes the stress off having to borrow them from the body's enzyme reserve, particularly from the white blood cell count (our immune system).

A most important point designated by Kautchakoff's experiment is that leukocytosis (increased white blood cell count) is a term which describes a medical pathology. Anytime the white blood cell count is increased to any great extent, it is considered that an acute illness or infection is present somewhere in the body. During acute diseases, enzyme levels rise. During chronic diseases, the body enzyme level is decreased. The pancreas and digestive tract are in a weakened state, as shown during diabetes, cancer, or chronic intestinal problems to name a few. During chronic disease, the immune system also shows signs of great expenditure. The correlation is clear. Enzymes are found to be related to all diseases via the immune system, whether the disease is acute or chronic. Our enzyme levels must be maintained at all expense to help maintain vitality, endurance, and to prevent disease. If the pancreas output of enzymes is hindered, the whole body is affected. If a disease is present, enzymes are being used up to fight the condition and the pancreas is affected. You can see how eating mostly cooked food all our lives, or trying to overcome a chronic disease while still eating this type of diet, can be detrimental.

ENDOCRINE SYSTEM AND ENZYMES

A cooked food diet not only kills the enzymes in food but causes the endocrine glands to become overworked and encourages the development of diseases such as hypo-glycemia and obesity. Columbus University published a paper entitled, "Comparative Experiments with Canned, Home Cooked and Raw Foods." The canned food, because of being cooked and/or preserved, is completely devoid of enzymes. It exerts a powerful stimulating effect on the endocrine glands, which can cause an increase in body weight. It has often been said that cooking makes food easier to digest and assimilate. This may be true, but if cooked food raises the white blood cell count, it can cause weight gain, and also robs the body of enzymes which otherwise would have been used to maintain metabolism. Therefore in the long run, it appears that it cannot be the best diet regimen to follow.

The endocrine system and the nervous system cooperate in regulating the appetite. The glands know when the body has had enough food and will shut off the food craving. Eating mostly raw food takes the stress off the endocrine system. Sugar and processed foods disrupt the endocrine balance because of their high caloric content. If the glands know the organism has had enough calories, but the nutrients and enzymes that usually accompany food aren't present because of being overcooked, the glands, not finding these nutrients, overstimulate the digestive organs, demanding more food than is needed to maintain strength and vitality. This results in the oversecretion of hormones, overeating, obesity, and finally exhaustion of the hormone-producing glands, not to mention the enzyme reserve it depletes trying to carry on the increased metabolic activity.

The false feeling of well-being is caused by the overstimulation of the pituitary gland. This gland is considered to be the master gland because it sends hormones to all of the other glands such as the thyroid, adrenals, reproductive glands, and pancreas. One can see the overshadowing damage that is done by eating enzymeless, overcooked food. Large amounts of enzymes are used up in this process, leaving the organs and tissues without their rightful share. By eating poorly, the breakdown and malfunction of organs not directly involved in digestion are hindered. Most diagnosticians are unaware of this fact. Since disease rarely involves just one or two organs, usually the entire body is affected. Enzymes, the circulatory system, nervous system, endocrine system, and the digestive system are connected and interdependent in life processes.

OBESITY AND CIRCULATORY DISEASES

Enzymes are not only important in terms of digestion, but also have other metabolic functions. They are found in tissues throughout the body, and when are found to be deficient in certain areas, it can be a major consideration in the cause of obesity and circulatory diseases. In observing enzyme therapy in different countries, it has been found that by administering enzymes during certain diseases positive results have been obtained.

Raw animal tissues and plants have sizeable amounts of lipase if unheated. It has been reported that in human obesity, the lipase content of the fatty tissue is decreased. Dr. David Galton of Tufts University, School of Medicine, examined eleven individuals weighing from 230-240 lbs. and found enzyme deficiencies in their fatty tissue. Not only the fatty tissues were found lacking lipase, but fatty tumors (lipomas) were also found deficient in lipase. (29) Lipase is the enzyme that aids the body in fat storage and the breaking down of fats. Animals in hibernation lose pounds of weight while sleeping because of lipase activity. Without lipase, fat stagnates and accumulates in the arteries, capillaries and other organs.

Why is there a deficiency of lipase in fatty tissues and in obese individuals? It is because when food is cooked, the lipase, which aids in fat digestion, and the burning of fat for energy and the storage and distribution of fat, is absent. Many experiments have been done to determine this. The problem is that these experiments were done using cooked food instead of raw food. This demonstrates only the fact that cooked calories put on weight, not necessarily raw food calories.

High caloric foods, such as meat and potatoes, have high enzyme values when raw. When cooked, these same foods provide little, if any, enzymes. Of course, many foods are not eaten in their raw state, although some Eskimos do eat their meat raw. After cooking, these foods have to be utilized by the body via enzymes. These enzymes are extracted from the body's own tissues. If there is an overabundance of cooked calories, they are stored in the body tissue as fat. This fat accumulates in the liver, kidneys, arteries, and capillaries. The stress on the body of enzymeless food not only causes an increase in body weight, but also the internal organs go through changes. A heat-treated, refined food diet causes drastic changes in the size and appearance of the pituitary gland. This relationship between enzymes and our glands was shown when the surgical removal of the glands in animals led to changes in the enzyme level of the blood.[30] Enzymes affect hormone-producing glands and hormones influence enzyme levels.

The glandular secretions of the pancreas and pituitary glands become exhausted from over-stimulation resulting from a cooked food diet. The body becomes sluggish, thyroid function also becomes exhausted, and weight is gained. Raw calories are relatively non-stimulating to glands and stabilize body weight. Farmers have proven this fact by feeding raw potatoes to hogs so they would not get fat. Cooking the potatoes, however, produced rapid weight gain in the hogs and they could be sold for more money. Think of the meat on the grocery shelves from animals like these with high fat content and low enzyme levels. Once cooked, you have less enzymes, and the fat is saturated, which is difficult to digest and finally accumulates in our arteries.

Dr. G.E. Burch at Tulane University demonstrated some interesting facts in the cause of obesity. He showed that young over-fed animals develop more fat cells than underfed ones.[31] Infants that are overfed can develop three times as many fat cells as is normal. When a normal person gains weight, he or she may get what is called pleasingly plump, but when a person who has been overfed as an infant and has accumulated many more fat cells and these cells are filled to an excess, obesity results. Both types of people can eat the same amount of food, but the one who has more fat cells and, consequently, more room to store fat, puts on weight much easier. A good way to help these people is to add raw foods to their diet with the addition of enzyme supplements. Personally, I lost 70 lbs. doing exactly this, and keeping my diet mostly raw, I haven't gained a pound in 12 years.

If one wants to reduce and keep his weight down, eating fewer meals per day will be beneficial. Frequent eating and snacking can decrease the enzyme level of the body and cause weight gain. In an experiment carried out at two different universities, the same results were found. Two groups of rats were used. One group was fed every two hours; the other, once a day. The rats that ate once a day lived seventeen percent longer, had lower body weight and higher enzyme activity in their pancreas and fat cells.[32] It is an important fact to remember that aging corresponds to diminishing enzyme levels. In this same experiment, it was found that enzyme activities in the tissues became weaker as the rats got older.

Enzyme deficiencies can also be the cause of circulatory and high blood pressure diseases and other blood vessel problems. In particular, the enzyme lipase is concerned in these diseases. Remember, lipase is the enzyme that digests, dissolves, and helps break down fats throughout the body. It has already been shown that younger people have a higher enzyme content in their blood and tissues than older folks. Doctors Berker and Meyers, found deficient lipase in individuals who had arteriosclerosis, high blood pressure, and slow fat absorption. Their investigations showed that the blood of individuals 77 years of age had only half the amount of blood lipase than the 27 year old group. Another observation made was that fat, not digested properly by lipase, can be absorbed in an undigested, adulterated state. This is found in the blood vessels and arteries, causing conditions such as arteriosclerosis (hardening of the arteries), high blood pressure, and high cholesterol. These fatty deposits clog the blood vessels and inhibit the blood from getting to the heart and can cause heart attacks. The heart has to work harder to push the blood through congested vessels which causes high blood pressure and an enlarged heart. The offenders to these problems are saturated fats (particularly from animal products), hydrogenated fats, and polyunsaturated fats. We have all been told that polyunsaturated fats lower cholesterol. This is true, but they work like a drug. In a fine book called *"The McDougall Plan"* it is stated that "polyunsaturated vegetable oils can be a health hazard. When consumed, they act like a cholesterol-lowering drug. They drive large amounts of stored cholesterol from the body tissues through the liver to the gall bladder and into the colon. In the bowel, the excreted cholesterol may be involved in the cause of cancer of the colon."[33] Rats fed on diets of cholesterol and polyunsaturated oils have more colon cancer than rats fed cholesterol and saturated fats. Although experiments with rats and other animals aren't always dependable, it is a well known fact that elements that cause cancer in animals also cause cancer in humans.

Fats impair the function of blood cells in the immune system by slowing down their circulation. This may be the reason why obese individuals seem to be prone to infections. High levels of fat in the blood also block the action of insulin which aids in the tissue absorption of sugar. This allows the sugar to rise in the blood which can be an attributing factor to diabetes.

Why do we find such a high percentage of circulatory diseases in civilized nations, and not in uncivilized groups of people? Primitive Eskimos who consume as much as ten pounds of meat daily, consisting of raw fish and blubber, have hardly any signs of circulatory diseases. The reason they don't develop vascular diseases is because most of their food is raw. The enzymes, in particular, lipase, are still active in the raw meat which aids in the prevention of circulatory diseases. At Stanford University, investigations showed that lipase was deficient in patients who had hardening of the arteries. The more advanced the case, the more a deficiency in enzymes was found. In another study, three British physicians demonstrated that in normal individuals, the enzyme lipase was found in blood serum. But in patients who had hardening of the arteries, they were found to be deficient in blood enzymes. When lipase was given to patients with slow fat metabolism and blood fat problems, there was an immediate improvement in fat metabolism.[34]

In wild animals and in primitive Eskimos who consume raw meat, the enzymes keep the arteries and capillaries clear of fatty deposits by promoting proper digestion and breakdown of fats, both in the digestive tract and in the liver. Dr. Maynard Murray, a Research Scientist, dissected over 3,000 whales who had a three to six inch layer of fat around their bodies. These whales had no signs of circulatory diseases. Their diet is raw fish. The same was found to be true in isolated Eskimos.

In 1926, Dr. William A. Thomas studied Eskimos who lived exclusively on raw meat and found no signs of kidney or vascular (blood vessel) diseases. In the adult Eskimos, aging from forty to sixty, the average blood pressure reading was 129/76. It should be remembered that these are primitive Eskimos. The more civilized Eskimos who settled in the Hudson Bay area, close to trading posts, used cooked food and white flour products. They gave up their primitive diet, and consequently their good health. You can now find arteriosclerosis and elevated blood pressure among these people. The only factor that was found to be different among the primitive and civilized Eskimos, was their diet.

Primitive Eskimos have a way of predigesting their food so when eaten, their body doesn't have to do all of the digestive work, thereby depleting their systems. They catch their fish live and bury it until it decays. All live tissue contains enzymes and these enzymes break down and predigest the food. The fish is then unearthed in this predigested state and is eaten. It is called "high fish" because it gives them strength and endurance. The body doesn't have to secrete large amounts of enzymes because the food is in this easily digestible state. Digestive energy is conserved, leaving more for work, metabolic functions, thinking and exercise. The Eskimos know that when they work their dogs for weeks, they become worn and tired. When fed just raw fish, the dogs became weak and thin, but when fed "high fish," they gain weight and strength.

This "pre-digestion" concept is not new. The Asiatic people have improved soybeans by adding enzymes from fungal plants to them, pre-digesting them and making foods common to the health food stores in the United States such as tofu, tempeh and miso. Cheeses and meats are aged by enzymes. In Lebanon, a dish of crushed raw lamb and wheat is let sit so that the enzymes predigest the food before it is eaten.

In summary, live food, uncooked, has its enzymes preserved. These enzymes not only predigest the food in fermentation processes, but also aid in digesting the food when eaten in its raw state. Within the blood stream and tissues of the body, enzymes act as scavengers, breaking down cholesterol and fatty deposits, assisting in the overall detoxification process. We are not saying that all food should be eaten raw by everybody, but a great majority of food should be. Studying the works of Viktoras Kulvinskas, author of *"Survival into the 21st Century,"* one can find information on raw food diets, sprouting, and predigested foods.

RAW FOOD DIET AND PREDIGESTION

It is a tremendous advantage to know how to use raw foods and supplemental enzymes in the diet. Well-known naturalists such as Arnold Ehret, Dr. Ann Wigmore, George J. Drews, and Viktoras Kulvinskas are people who have shown the healing effects of raw foods. It is a fact that the enzymes in foods aid in digestion. This enzyme activity takes place in what Dr. Howell has called the enzyme-stomach, or the upper part of the stomach. Anatomically speaking it is called the cardial and fundic parts of the stomach. Here is where foods are predigested by enzymes. I will refer to the upper portion of the stomach as the enzyme-stomach. (See Diagram 2)

The enzyme stomach is not original to the human race. Cattle and sheep have no enzymes in their saliva, but have four stomachs. Only one secretes enzymes; the other stomachs let the enzymes within the food do the partial-digesting or predigesting. Dolphins and whales have three stomachs. One is devoid of enzymes when the food enzymes do the predigesting. There has been as many as thirty-two seals found in the enzyme-stomach of one whale at one time. Since there is no enzyme secretion in this stomach, how does all of the flesh get broken down into small enough amounts in order to pass the small opening which connects the enzyme-stomach to the other stomachs? The enzymes contained in the flesh of the eaten animal itself seems to be the only answer.

After the death of animal bodies, the tissues become acidic. This acid releases an enzyme called cathepsin which begins the predigestion of the flesh protein. This enzyme and others predigest the food and remain active for long periods of time. The whale, or other animals that have consumed their food, benefit tremendously from this predigestion. Their bodies do

DIAGRAM 2

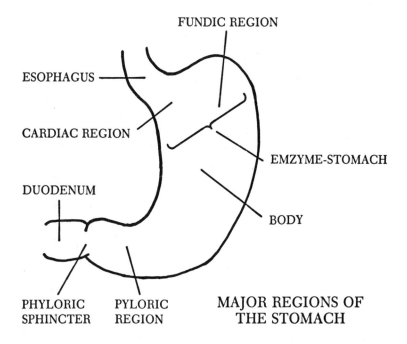

FUNDIC REGION

ESOPHAGUS

CARDIAC REGION

EMZYME-STOMACH

DUODENUM

BODY

PHYLORIC
SPHINCTER

PYLORIC
REGION

MAJOR REGIONS OF
THE STOMACH

not have to secrete large amounts of enzymes to digest the food.

We have already shown that enzymes help digest the food they are contained in if not destroyed by heat during cooking. These enzymes not only work in the stomach, but continue their activity in the small intestine. Popular opinion seems to be that the acid in the stomach destroys the enzymes in food. Research has shown this to be untrue. North Western University has shown that supplemental enzymes pass through the stomach uninjured. In one study the enzyme, amylase, from germinated barley, digested starch in the stomach and then passed into the small intestine where it continued digestion.

It was also thought that only protein was digested in the stomach. Research by Dr. Beazell in the "Journal of Laboratory and Clinical Medicine," showed that several times more starch was digested in the stomach than protein within the first hour. Olaf Berglim, Professor of Physiology at the Illinois College of Medicine, has also shown this to be true. He gave his subjects mashed potatoes and bread as a meal. Both foods contain large amounts of starch. After remaining in the stomach for 45 minutes, the contents were retrieved. Seventy-six percent of the starch in the mashed potatoes was digested and fifty-nine percent of the bread starch was digested. Research has shown that for the first forty-five minutes to one hour, a good percentage of food can be predigested in the stomach by food enzymes or supplemental enzymes before reaching the small intestine. At this time, the pancreas secretes its protein, fat, and starch-digestive enzymes into the duodenum (the first part of the small intestine). The pancreas can be put under tremendous stress if the food is not properly predigested at this point. It has to draw enzymes from the whole body to secrete the designated amount. The more digestion that takes place before the food reaches the small intestine, the better for the integrity, strength, and immunity of the whole body. The pancreas is one of the first organs to dysfunction during diabetes and other chronic illnesses.

The importance of this food-enzyme stomach, where predigestion takes place, cannot be overestimated. It is the upper part of the stomach where no acid secretion or peristalsis takes place for one-half to one hour after food is eaten. This is when supplemental enzymes and the natural enzymes contained in food do their predigestion.

Gray's Anatomy cites the authority Walter B. Cannon who demonstrated that the human stomach "consists of two parts physiologically distinct." Gray's Anatomy states:

"The cardiac portion of the stomach is a food reservoir in which salivary digestion continues; the pyloric portion is the seat of active gastric digestion. There are no peristaltic waves in the cardiac portion."

Predigestion by exogenous (outside) enzymes is widespread in nature. Our enzyme potential has other and more useful and taxing work to do than merely making endogenous digestive enzymes to digest food.[35]

The body is greatly relieved when predigestion takes place.

The draw on metabolic enzymes is kept at a minimum. There is a law called the "Adaptive Secretion of Digestive Enzymes." This means that the more digestion that is accomplished by food enzymes or supplemental enzymes in the stomach, the less needs to be secreted by the pancreas and intestines, conserving the body's enzymes for metabolic processes such as repairing tissues, organs, and other functions.

If the food is over-cooked and the enzymes destroyed, the only enzymes that get mixed with the food are the ones contained in saliva. Some starch digestion may take place in the stomach from the saliva amylase. The protein is acted upon by the stomach pepsin, but mostly in the lower part of the stomach. In both instances, no help from outside enzymes is being demonstrated. The fat remains practically untouched only to wait until it moves into the small intestine for the pancreatic secretions of lipase. The food remains in the food-enzyme stomach for its allotted time and practically no pre-digestion takes place, except for the starch. Cooked foods, especially those high in protein, can begin putrifying. The by-products of putrification are toxins that are absorbed into the bloodstream and deposited at body sites far removed from the intestinal tract. At this point, one can see how valuable enzymes are in helping to keep the blood clear of poisons. It has been estimated that 80 % of diseases are caused by improperly digested foods and their by-products being absorbed into the body.[36]

A diet containing mostly cooked food has proven to be detrimental in more ways than one.

Cooking does not improve the nutritional value of food. It destroys or makes unavailable 85 % of the original nutrients. Cooked food is totally lacking in enzymes; most of the protein has been destroyed or converted to new forms which are either not digestible by body enzymes or digested with difficulty; many of the vitamins have lost their vitality. To purchase organic food and then to waste precious hours in destroying most of the nutrients is poor economy and unsound ecology. Francis Pottenger, M.D., carried out a 10-year experiment using 900 cats which were placed on controlled diets. The cats on raw food produced healthy kittens from generation to generation. Those on cooked food developed our modern ailments: heart, kidney and thyroid disease, pneumonia, paralysis, loss of teeth, difficulty in labor, diminished or perverted sexual interest, diarrhea, irritability. Liver impairment on cooked protein was progressive, the bile in the stool becoming so toxic that even weeds refused to grow in soil fertilized by the cats' excrement. The first generation of kittens were sick and abnormal; the second generation were often born dead or diseased; by the third generation, the mother was sterile.[37]

Zoologists know that captured animals fed a human diet develop human diseases such as gastritis, duodenitis, colitis, liver diseases, anemia, thyroid diseases, arthritis and circulatory problems. I am not stating that everybody should exist on a raw food diet. Some individuals don't have the inclination nor the interest to even try, but improving one's diet by taking supplemental enzymes or eating a good quantity of predigested foods, can be beneficial. Naturally, predigested foods include sprouts and fruits. This means that the proteins, starches and fats are already predigested and high in enzymes before they are consumed. Sprouting seeds is simple and beneficial to your health. There are several books in health food stores which can explain sprouting procedures.

BODY, MIND AND ENZYMES

Since it seems that our happiness depends largely upon the thoughts we think, it is impossible to think positively at all times when we are toxic, stiff, and are experiencing low blood sugar levels. Our brain exists on large amounts of sugar and oxygen. When this supply is low, we experience a lack of concentration, insomnia, lethargy, irritability and confusion.

A lack of enzymes, oxygen, and sugar supplies to the cells of our body can cause hypoglycemia. Hypoglycemia is a disorder resulting from too low blood sugar, which is the fuel for our cells. Authorities have estimated that anywhere from *ten* to *one-hundred million Americans* are suffering from hypoglycemia. Since hypoglycemia is a malfunction of our fuel supply, every organ is then affected. Here's how: as the sugar level drops, the metabolism of every organ drops, resulting in fatigue and psychosomatic problems. The brain is nourished exclusively by glucose and oxygen. A drop in one's blood sugar can cause mental fatigue and depression. The endocrine glands, especially the pituitary, adrenals, thyroid, and pancreas, control the sugar level. The pancreas secretes insulin which causes a decrease in blood sugar. Insulin facilitates the movement of glucose (blood sugar) to leave the blood and enter the cells. Insulin also stimulates the liver and muscle cells to convert glucose into glycogen, which is a carbohydrate and the chief storage compound of sugar in the body. The adrenal glands secrete a hormone called epinephrine that when stimulated causes the stored sugar (glycogen) to break down into glucose which then enters the blood to raise the blood sugar. The thyroid gland secretes hormones that control the rate at which the body uses oxygen. Also its hormones increase the rate of energy released from carbohydrates. All of these glands are controlled by the pituitary gland, which, in turn, is controlled by an area of the brain called the hypothalamus. The hypothalamus receives information from all parts of the body via the nervous system. This includes (whether he is hungry or not) a person's emotional state, body temperature, blood nutrient concentration, among other things.

It has been shown that the pituitary and other organs can enlarge, become exhausted, and then be susceptible to disease when a deficiency of enzymes is present. When there is a lack of blood amylase, blood sugar levels can be higher than normal. With the addition of the enzyme amylase, blood sugar levels have been lowered. In experiments done by Grubler and Myers, they showed that by giving amylase preparations to normal individuals after eating 80 grams of glucose, the blood sugar level was maintained.[38] Reports have shown that oral or intravenous injection of amylase causes a lowering of blood sugar levels in diabetics. Bassler showed that 86% of the diabetics that he examined had a deficiency of amylase in their intestinal secretions. After administering amylase to a majority of these patients, 50% of the diabetics who were users of insulin could control their blood sugar levels without the use of insulin.[39] Amylase seems to help the storage and utilization of sugar in the blood.

Cooked food, where most of the amylase and other enzymes are destroyed, has a tremendous effect on the blood sugar levels. At George Washington University Hospital, 50 grams of raw starch were fed to hospital patients. The blood sugar showed an average increase of 1 mg. per 100 cc. in one-half hour, a decrease of 1.2 mg. in one hour, and a decrease of 3 mg. in two hours. When 50 grams of cooked starch was given, the average increase in blood sugar was 56 mg. in one-half hour, then dropped to 51 mg. in one hour, then down to 11 mg. in two hours after eating the meal. In the diagram below notice the difference between the blood sugar levels when cooked and when raw starch with the enzymes present, is eaten. The blood sugar in cooked starch rose to 56 mg. in one-half hour opposed to the uncooked starch increase of only 1 mg. After two hours, the cooked food starch eaters' blood sugar level fell to 11 mg., a 45 mg. drop in blood sugar. This resulted in fatigue, anxiety, and the other aforementioned symptoms. The raw starch eaters only experienced a drop of 1 mg. to 3 mg. in two hours. A much more steady metabolic rate and emotional stability was experienced by the raw food eaters.

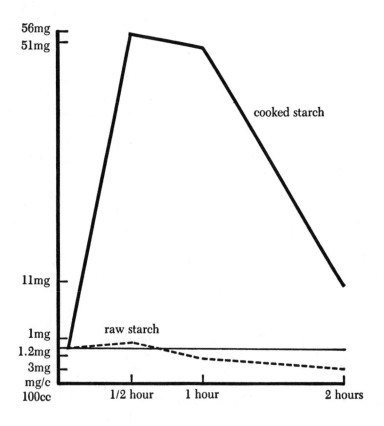

The endocrine glands need trace minerals and vitamins to function properly. A similar example of this is that of the thyroid gland needing iodine, and the adrenal glands needing vitamin C. Overcooked food is deficient not only in enzymes, but in nutrients also. These deficiencies cause many problems. The glands of the body are controlled by stimuli from the brain to secrete their hormones. When the blood sugar level drops below normal, the pancreas and adrenal glands are called upon to secrete their hormones. When there is a lack of nutrients in the blood which support the endocrine glands, the hypothalamus stimulates the appetite and causes a craving for food. The more that cooked food is eaten the more there will be hormone stimulation, resulting in overeating. Excessive eating can cause one to be overweight and obese. Obesity can be the cause of heart problems, high blood pressure and many other diseases. Quick rising and falling blood sugar levels in the body cause emotional swings and mental imbalances. Finally, the endocrine glands, deficient in their secretions from trying to keep the body metabolism normal, become exhausted. This state of exhaustion can be the foundation of both mental and physical diseases.

Enzymes have as much to do with our mental and physical health as any other considered element of nutrition. This is a subject that has not been given enough attention in today's literature. I hope this book will enlighten you as to the importance of food enzymes in your system as well as bring it to the public's eye.

DETOXIFICATION AND ENZYMES

There are several methods that have been used to detoxify the body: fasting, purging, vegetarian-type diets, macrobiotic diets, the grape cure and others. All of these have been successful to some on their own. At the same time none of these regimes will work all the time. The question is, what can be done to improve all of these methods of cleansing the body to make them more proficient?

Anytime cooked food is eaten it must be digested by enzymes. The waste left over from the digestion of these foods and the toxins contained within the foods themselves, are broken down by scavenger enzymes in the body's immune system. The body draws enzymes from all of its tissue resources to do the job, decreasing its enzyme level. Concentrated foods such as heavy starches (breads and flour products), animal proteins, and fried foods, are more difficult to break down and consequently more enzymes are utilized. This is why, in most situations, a vegetarian diet is used for cleansing purposes. A good percentage of these diets are raw, which add some enzymes to the body and to the food-enzyme stomach. Cooked vegetables and grains use some of the body's enzymes but are still easier to digest than more concentrated foods. The energy that is used to digest food and extract the nutrients, and eliminate the waste products while on a cleansing diet (especially if raw juices and predigested foods are used), is far less than the energy used to digest the everyday, traditional enzymeless diet. I have seen tremendous recoveries on predigested food diets that consist of raw sprouts, freshly-squeezed juices, fasting, soaked and sprouted grains and soaked seeds and nuts that are blended before being eaten.

Two major changes take place in predigested foods: 1) the

enzyme content sometimes increases 10-fold and 2) in the predigestion process the food is broken down into simpler components. Proteins are broken down into amino acids, starches into simpler sugars, and fats into fatty acids. This relieves the body of breaking down the more concentrated food elements and it also benefits from the increase in enzymes. This is conserving energy and enzymes for other metabolic functions. In other words, more energy and enzymes can be used in the healing process.

In the detoxification process, what we are trying to accomplish is the purification of the blood stream and the balancing of the endocrine glands so that they will work in harmony instead of being overstimulated and exhausted. This purifies the organs and tissues, and takes the stress off the entire body. The foods that do not get digested properly can cause toxic reactions. For example, Dr. W.W. Oelgoetz had shown that undigested protein, fat, and starch molecules get absorbed into the bloodstream, and when the blood enzyme level is below normal, these obstructions can cause allergies. By giving the enzymes amylase, protease, and lipase orally to his patients, the blood enzyme level was normalized and alleviated the allergies.[40] I can personally verify this, having had a history of numerous allergies as a result of living on a traditional Italian diet. I switched to a vegetarian diet and before long, my allergies were gone.

We have discussed that enzymes are a part of our immune system. We also showed that when there is a lack of lipase in the blood, cholesterol can accumulate. When there is a shortage of amylase, there can be sugar level problems and drastic emotional swings. So there is no need, at that point, to prove that enzymes are used for breakdown of toxins and foreign accumulation in our bodies. It would seem logical then that any diet that would increase the enzyme level would aid the purification process, especially when we now know that enzymes can be reabsorbed and reused in the body.

Much has been written about the so-called "healing crisis"—myself included. I have discussed this topic thoroughly in my book "*Natural Healing with Herbs,*" published by Hohm Press. The "healing crisis" occurs when the system is overloaded with toxins and the body works to eliminate them through the skin, bowels, sinuses, kidneys, and lungs, producing such symtoms as rashes, lung and sinus congestion, constipation and diarrhea, and urinary tract problems. All of these can be symptoms of body cleansing. During these crises, enzymes are busy breaking down the accumulations of waste so that the body can rid itself of them. By adding enzymes during the crises, it would seem that it could only be an improvement and ultimately aid in the cleansing process. This has proven to be true in nature. For those who wish to do more research into this topic, you may find great benefits by reading *"Food Enzymes for Health and Longevity"* and *"Enzyme Nutrition"* by Dr. Edward Howell.

There are times when detoxification actually weakens the patient, even though a good cleansing diet has been prescribed. The tissues, releasing poisons that have been stored for years, may contain drugs that were ingested years before. If patients have a weak constitution, a chronic disease, and a submissive will, as soon as the first healing crisis is experienced, they tend to go back to their old diet thinking that the cleansing diet isn't worth it because it makes them feel worse, even if only temporarily. These people really are in need of enzyme support. Taking supplemental enzymes and using predigested foods will take much of the stress off their systems. They also need a good learning process in relation to proper eating habits, fasting, and the *proper* use of colonics and enemas. All of these things are adjuncts to healing. Bowel cleansing is one of the first things considered by natural healing practitioners. The bowel is the sewage system of the body and it too must be cleansed out. It has been estimated that 80% of all diseases start in the large bowel. What generally happens is that food that is not digested putrifies in the colon, producing byproducts that are reabsorbed through the intestinal tract and deposited in the joints and tissues of the body. It has been shown by Dr. Selle that by adding enzymes to the diet, the fecal bulk is reduced, transit time is speeded up, and the nitrogen compounds found in high protein foods that putrify into toxic gases can be reduced from 30 to 60%.[41]

When poisons are eliminated from the tissues they then enter the blood stream. These poisons cause the endocrine glands to secrete hormones which in turn stimulate the eliminative organs and result in a feeling of stimulation. When the glands become overworked and exhausted, there will be a feeling of exhaustion and recovery time will be necessary.

The point here is that enzymes can be used not only to maintain health, but also be used during detoxification programs. Enzymes can be used in both medical and non-medical approaches to healing. They can be the support system to all systems and to health-promotion processes.

There are many enzyme supplements on the market today. Some are better than others. Finding the most suitable enzymes, those being ones that can be substituted for the lack of body enzymes, are of primary importance. Since digestion takes place in the stomach and in the small intestine, enzymes that have activity in both areas will aid the body more than ones that work in just one of these organs. The stomach and small intestine are where most of the digestion takes place. Both areas have different pH's, consequently, enzymes that can do their digestion in a wider range of pH are much more beneficial.

What is pH? Acid and alkaline are two words used to describe degrees of pH. PH means hydrogen potential. The more hydrogen there is in the solution, the more acidic it is. As the hydrogen concentration decreases, the more alkaline a solution becomes. So, acid and alkaline, in reality, are describing the hydrogen concentration in a solution. Numbers indicate pH ranges. The pH range is from 1 to 14: 1 to 6 is acidic, 1 being very acidic, 6 being only slightly acidic; 7 is neutral; and 8 to 14 indicate that the solution is becoming more and more alkaline.

The body's digestive juices contain pH ranges. Protein digestion is partially accomplished in the stomach where hydrochloric acid is secreted along with the digestive juices creating a pH between 1.6 and 4.0. When protein and other food substances are partially digested and become a semi-fluid paste called chyme, it passes slowly into the small intestine. This chyme has acid pH. In the first part of the small intestine (duodenum) it is neutralized by the pancreatic secretions which contain bi-carbonate ions. This secretion changes the pH from acid to more alkaline (a pH of around 7 to 8). This action is important because pancreatic and intestinal enzymes function best in an alkaline environment.

Pepsin is an enzyme that is secreted in the stomach that begins digestion of protein foods. It can only function in an acid digestive juice. When it enters the small intestine, its action is blocked by the neutrality of pancreatic alkaline secretions. At this point, trypsin, a pancreatic enzyme, is secreted in the small intestine which also digests protein. It more or less takes over where pepsin leaves off. So, the body digests protein in the stomach in an acid environment then continues in the small intestine in an alkaline environment. The pancreas also secretes amylase and lipase in the small intestine to digest fats and carbohydrates.

For years enzymes have been extracted from the intestines and pancreases of animals, put into tablets and taken orally to aid the digestive process. It has been postulated that enzymes extracted from plants did not have the capabilities of substituting for these tissue enzyme extracts. Dr. Howell and other scientists have proven otherwise.

An interesting research paper was published by the Biochemical Department of E. Merch by Hinnrich, Huffmann and Lang entitled, "Suitability of the Plant Protease Bromelin for Substitution Therapy in Interestinal Disorders." The digestive capabilities of bromelin, and enzyme extracted from pineapples, and the body's own enzymes, pepsin and trypsin were compared. Dr. W.H. Taylor of the University of Oxford, investigated the digestive pH of the stomach. He found there to be two pH zones. At the beginning of protein digestion in the enzyme-stomach, the pH ranges from 3.4 to 4.0. As digestion continues, the pH becomes more acidic ranging from approximately 1.6 to 2.4

In this research paper, Dr. Taylor stated that the body's enzyme pepsin functions best in a pH between 1.5 and 2.5. This means that at the beginning of digestion in the stomach, when the pH is 3 to 4, pepsin is not at its optimum digestive capability. In other words, when the food is in the predigestion-stomach, pepsin has little activity. As the stomach becomes more acidic, in approximately 1/2 to 1 hour after food is eaten, pepsin's activity increases. On the other hand, bromelin was found to be active in a pH range of 3 to 8. It was not only found active in the stomach's higher pH ranges (from 3 to 4), but was also found in the small intestine still actively digesting protein in an alkaline environment (approximately 7 to 8). This again, exemplifies the truth that some enzymes do survive the acid secretions of the stomach.

As previously stated, the pancreas creates an alkaline environment in the duodenum (first part of the small intestine) with its secretions. Also, it secretes its enzyme, trypsin, that continues protein digestion in the small intestine in an alkaline environment. Bromelin was shown to have the same digestive capabilities as pepsin and trypsin. It has a double effect, both in the stomach and intestines. Thus, it is said that bromelin can be effectively substituted for pepsin and trypsin in enzyme supplementation.

Another misconception is that the only food that gets partially digested in the stomach is protein, leaving fat and carbohydrate digestion up to the pancreatic secretions in the small intestine. It has been established that the enzymes in plants can function in a wide pH range and that they can carry on their activity both in the stomach and small intestine, predigesting starches and fats. The enzymes I am speaking of are not just proteolytic enzymes, but also fat and carbohydrate digestive enzymes. Dr. Selle, a physiologist from the University of Texas, fed dogs cereal starch with the addition of the starch digestive enzyme amylase, extracted from barley. The pancreases of the dogs were ligated (tied off) so that no pancreatic digestive juices would affect digestion. The stomachs were then emptied after a certain period of time and in some cases, the cereal starch was 65% digested. The barley amylase was proven to digest the starch in the stomach in pH's as acidic as 2.5. When ptylin (the starch digestive enzyme in human saliva) was compared to this amylase, it was found to be inactivated in the stomach at a 4.5 pH. The ptylin could not function in an acidic pH as well as the plant amylase did. To prove that plant amylase was so effective: one-half hour after it was orally taken, 69-71% of it was found in the small intestine still actively digesting starch. When the fecal matter was studied for its enzyme content, to see if the plant amylse could be found, there was a larger amount of plant amylase than the body's own pancreatic enzymes.[42] At this point, I would like to point out that enzymes from fungus (mushrooms and yeast) were experimented with and they also were found to be very active in both the stomach and intestines, and still found to be active in the large intestine.

The starch amylase is not the only enzyme that can function throughout the digestive tract. Plant proteases and lipase can function at a 3 to 8.5 pH, so they can actively continue digestion in both the stomach and small intestine.

Enzymes are needed that can work in the predigestive areas of the stomach, in an acid pH in the lower part of the stomach and in the alkaline environment, as found in the small intestine. Dr. Howell, after years of research, found that the enzymes in certain fungus, if cultured on food materials such as wheat, bran, or soybeans, have the enzymes protease, lipase, amylase, and cellulase. These enzymes can function in tremendously wide pH ranges. They have been found to function throughout the whole intestinal tract, also helping increase deficient blood enzyme patterns. He states that chewing a few of these capsulated enzymes with meals, or taking the powder in small amounts of water before eating, is best. Here is a chart comparing and demonstrating the ranges of pH that these enzymes function best in:

EFFECTIVE pH RANGES

(Contains lipase, protease, and amylase)

You can see that pancreation cannot function in a wide range of pH. Pancreation is a term used to describe the pancreatic digestive secretions containing lipase, protease, and amylase. These enzymes are secreted by human and animal pancreases. Usually they are extracted, purified and concentrated from slaughterhouse animals. The fault with them is that they can only function in the small intestine where the pH is slightly alkaline. As a supplement, they cannot function in the predigestive stomach where much of the digestion can take place. Usually, these supplemental pancreatic enzymes (pancreatin) are contained in enteric capsules (capsules treated in such a way as to pass through the stomach unaltered and disintegrated in the intestines). These capsules cannot dissolve in the acidity of the stomach. The alkaline juices from the pancreas dissolve the enteric coating and release the enzymes in the small intestine. The enteric-coated capsules do not work at all in the predigestive stomach. Furthermore, their release is triggered by the pancreatic secretion which does not take the stress off the pancreas as much as the plant enzymes do. This is because the plant enzymes have predigested a good percentage of the food in the stomach and have begun digesting in the small intestine before the pancreas secretes its enzymes. Hence, the pancreas secretes less of its enzymes because much of the digestion has already taken place. This leaves more enzymes in the body for metabolic functions and body repairs.

The enzymes from certain plants break down and digest food elements through the whole digestive tract. By the time the food gets down into the small intestine, the pancreas has less work to do, secreting smaller amounts of enzymes. This is a relief to the whole body. These enzymes can be found in most health food stores.

Another point is that when raw foods are eaten, less stomach acid is secreted than when cooked food is eaten, which gives the enzymes contained in the raw food more time for predigestion. When raw food is eaten, the enzymes are attached to their substrate which protects them from acid digestive juices so that they can function better. If the food is cooked and the enzymes are destroyed, the substrate remains inactive in the predigestive stomach. If the food substrate is a fat or starch, it must wait until it passes into the small intestine before most of the digestion takes place. Oftentimes, when the digestion is sluggish, or the enzyme level is low, as found in elderly folks, the food ferments and causes gas, bloating, constipation, colitis and other problems.

Having an understanding of these facts permits our logic to tell us that a vegetarian diet with at least 75% raw food, is favorable. If this amount of raw food cannot be tolerated, plant enzyme supplements can be used. Even if all raw food diet is eaten, the proper amount of enzymes may not be guaranteed because citrus fruits and non-starchy vegetables have small amounts of enzymes when compared to starchy, raw foods like bananas, mangos, and avocados. So, we can see that even the raw foodist can benefit from taking enzymes extracted from plant sources.

CHILDREN AND ENZYMES

As previously pointed out, many diseases in their early stages of development have two major causes. The first is the ingestion of enzyme-deficient foods over a period of time, coupled with eating foods that lack the vitamins and minerals needed daily. Manufacturing procedures, mineral-depleted soils, and cooked, enzymeless foods create this undernutrition. The second cause is carcinogens, cholesterol, x-rays, drugs, caffeine, and other life-impinging agents used throughout our lifetime. Our children are equally affected by both.

One of the first questions asked is, "How are babies born with health problems?" Complete breast-feeding of infants is of very great importance. Mother's milk has all of the nutrients needed for the growth of the child and a large amount of live enzymes which the baby thrives on. Milk formulas lack enzymes and other artificial formulas can be toxic to the child, causing infections, mucus conditions, fevers, diarrhea, colic, and allergies. At the Infant Welfare Centre of Chicago, over a period of years, the health and development of 20,061 infants was closely monitored for the first nine months of the infant's life. Of these, 48.5% were wholly breastfed, 43% partially breast-fed, and 8.5% wholly artificially fed. The mortality rates of these different groups were as follows:

	No. of Infants	Total Deaths	% of Death of Infants
Wholly Breast-Fed	9,749	15	0.15
Partially	8,605	59	.7
Artificially	1,707	144	8.4

The mortality rate among the artificially fed infants was *fifty-six times greater* than among the breast-fed. Four of the 9,749 breast-fed infants died of respiratory infections, compared to eighty-two of the 1,707 artificially-fed infants. In the United States one deformed child is born every 5 minutes, which is the equivalent of one in every ten families. In this country alone we are producing 250,000 deformed infants yearly. Seventy-five percent have mental defects.

There are two major factors involved when considering children's health. The first, of course, is the mother's health. Dr. Bieler, M.D., states "that unless the mother is detoxified before conceiving, the baby comes into the world...full of toxins from the mother's blood and an intestine full of meconium (black bile). The baby is, in fact, so toxic that even with the best care it usually takes three years to eliminate his or her inherited birth poisons." The second point to be considered here is that once a child has been brought into this world with a weak constitution, and a bloodstream ladened with poison, he or she is then expected to exist on a diet of concentrated, enzymeless foods. Heavy starches and mucus-inducing foods (dairy products, grains, sugar, bread) bring on respiratory disorders, asthma, pneumonia, measles, and runny noses. Eating excessively fatty foods brings on high cholesterol problems, acne, and boils. Just recently (1986), doctors have begun to examine school children for high cholesterol and triglycerides. The foods most school children consume lack the three major enzymes, lipase, protease, and amylase that help break down foods in the digestive tract. This results in the absorption of large protein and fat molecules which lay the foundation for allegies, obesity, constipation and fatigue.

There are two major problems that the school systems must cope with: hyperactivity of chldren and absenteeism. It is very difficult for children to learn valuable information when they cannot concentrate. Read again the section in this book on "Body, Mind, and Enzymes." The relationship between the mind and what a person eats is of paramount importance. Learning disabilities are often caused by nutrient deficiencies. The majority of deficiencies are caused by foods that lack enzymes—too much cooked food, junk food, processed food, etc. The child's body becomes toxic and the nerves become irritated. Two children out of every 100 have a neurological disorder. These are disorders that are observed by medical examinations. What about the hyperactive child that doesn't exhibit a true physiological disorder but suffers from an overstimulated nervous system caused by soft drinks, caffeine in chocolate bars, sugar, or other stimulants? Haven't you ever experienced the jitters when you had too much coffee or too much sugar? Consider that a child's body is much more sensitive than our own. In some cases even just the use of salt can cause hyperactivity, dehydration, and allergies.

To show how important enzymes are, an experiment was performed at Washington University. Surgeons equipped a group of dogs with tubes designed to drain all of the pancreatic juice enzymes out of the body so that the enzymes could not be utilized. Despite the animals' usual access to food and water, profound deterioration set in, and all of them died within a week. The importance of enzymes cannot be overemphasized. If the lack of enzymes can cause disease, then adding enzymes to the diet, either by supplementation or by eating proper food, would help to prevent disease. Adding enzymes to one's diet is the logical thing to do when we consider that enzymes are used up daily. Children that maintain high enzyme levels maintain high energy levels. Consider the many ways young adults and growing children lose enzymes. During all fevers and infections, the immune system uses large amounts of enzymes to protect the body and to eliminate toxins and bacteria. In fact, as previously stated, anytime the temperature of the body is raised, enzymes are used up— both during healthy exercise as well as during fever. More calories are being burnt during exercise and this natural oxidation process is initiated by enzymes.

Over-feeding a child, especially with cooked, devitalized food, causes the digestive organs to secrete large amounts of enzymes daily, which over a period of time can exhaust the enzyme-producing organs and deplete the immunity of the whole body. This puts a strain on every tissue throughout the body. This child will tend to act exhausted, as compared to peers, because his or her energy is being used for digesting foods and coping with the large amounts of waste left over from the unnaturally large food supplies. The body is then required to store large amounts of fat which puts an additional strain on the heart, kidneys, and lungs.

It should be clear that we use up our given amount of enzymes in many different ways. The proper thing to do is to feed your child and yourself only when you are hungry. This will conserve enzymes. You and your child should eat most of your food raw and add enzyme supplements to enhance digestion. Consider occasional, short fasts. During fasting the enzymes go to work cleaning up undigested materials in the blood and purifying the whole body. Then resume a good healthy diet cutting out the junk food and increase the fresh fruit and vegetables.

THE USE OF ENZYMES IN THE PREVENTION OF ALLERGIES AND CANDIDA

In natural therapeutics, all diseases are considered to be systematic problems. This means that all body processes are involved. To bring about favorable results, the whole body must be influenced in a positive direction. In considering candida and allergies there are many similarities between the two, both in cause and prevention. Basically the symptoms of both maladies are caused by the body's attempt to resist the organisms or toxins that tend to damage tissues and organs. This capacity is called immunity. In this section I will discuss basic immune responses of these conditions and how to aid the immune system in preventing such problems.

A major part of our immune system consists of several types of white blood cells such as lymphocytes, macrophages, T-cells, B-cells and neutrophils. T-cells get their name becuse the thymus gland aids in their production. B-cells are named after tiny little sacs in the body called "bursa" where they migrate to be processed until maturity. T- and B-cells are lymphocytes but they differ slightly in their duties. T-Lymphocytes become sensitized to specific toxins or antigens (substances that cause immune responses, such as toxins, drugs, among a few) and attack them whenever they enter the body. B-Lymphocytes produce antibodies which are molecules that react with certain antigens in the body aiding in their destruction.

The white blood cells help to destroy antigens and other toxins by engulfing them and digesting or partically destroying their substance making it easier for the body to eliminate them. In most cases, they do this by secreting enzymes that break down the antigens. As previously mentioned, different research experiments that were performed by Dr. Willstatter as far back as 1929 and proved that white blood cells contain eight different types of amylase, protease, and lipase. He states that "white blood cells provide transportation for enzymes throughout the body."

Antigens, bacteria, yeast, and other toxins enter the body through the digestive tract. They leech onto food substances we ingest and then multiply prolifically within the body of the immune system if it is not strong and healthy enough to destroy them. Allergens (substances causing the allergy) can also enter the body simply through the air that we breath. Most antigens, bacteria, viruses and yeasts are proteins. Often the toxins that are causing allergies and infections are secreted by bacteria which also contain protein substances. At this point it can be understood that the body needs a tremendous supply of protease (protein digestive enzymes) to counteract the constant bombardment of these proteins to digest and eliminate them. This digestion of protein is done by enzymes, not only in the digestive tract, but in the bloodstream itself. Undigested proteins are often found in the bloodstream. If digestion is not properly accomplished, undigested substances can be absorbed through the digestive tract. Antigens that cause allergies attach themselves to these proteins in the blood (antigen complex), deposit in the walls of tiny capillaries and secrete substances that cause inflammations which result in swellings, sneezing, hayfever, hives, asthma, etc. In order for the body to rid itself of the allergen it must be separated from the protein molecule. This is accomplished by enzymes that digest the protein and release the allergen so the body can eliminate it via the lymphatic system. This is why it is so important to keep the lymphatic system clean. Echinacea is an herb that is a specific lymphatic cleanser. It is an excellent herb to use to combat allergies in combination with enzymes because it stimulates the production of white blood cells, and is used to treat inflammations, lymphatic swellings, and infections.

The importance of understanding why undigested proteins, bacteria and yeast entering the blood via the intestinal wall have toxic effects on one's system, cannot be stressed strongly enough. Their quick and proliferate spreading often leaves the body with numerous symptoms and physical indications. Candida Albicans, which lives practically everywhere in the body, is an example of such a yeast. These yeasts live naturally in the intestinal tract and vaginal areas of animals and human beings. They can take over our whole body if the immunity is weakened. It is important to realize that yeasts are also protein bodies and can be digested by enzymes if the body has a proper supply.

Candida can change form in the human intestines. It can remain in a yeast-fungal form and enter the circulation or develop a root structure that penetrates the intestines which creates a large enough opening for other bacteria, antigens, and undigested protein to enter. These other substances that enter are a major cause of allergies, anxiety, fatigue, digestive disturbances, vaginitis, cystitis, menstrual problems and migraine headaches. This is the reason for the similar approach in treating both candida and allergies.

Yeast and most antigens (being protein bodies) can be eliminated by administering supplemental enzymes. This nourishes the white blood cells which causes a direct improvement of the immune system. Some allergies are not in themselves protein bodies. They attach to protein molecules and must be split off from the molecule by proteolytic enzymes and then be eliminated by the lymphatic system.

Undigested proteins that yeast and other allergens attach themselves to in the circulation often enter through the digestive tract. One way to prevent this is to take plant enzymes with meals to aid in the digestion of these substances.

An effective approach to candida, allergies, or any other systematic problems is to take plant enzymes between meals and thereby help to increase the enzyme activity through the whole body, and reestablish these levels both in the digestive tract and the bloodstream. Again, simply eating larger amounts of raw foods which have the enzymes still present, taking supplemental enzymes, and additionally using echinacea can help alleviate problems of this type. Also, using lactobacillus acidophilus will help check the spreading of yeast in the intestines and also nourish the immune system.

SPORTS — ENZYMES — AND NUTRITION

An athlete's main concern should be the type of food he eats in order to maintain a healthy body and to replace the nutrients which are lost during exercise or competition. Enzymes, carbohydrates, proteins, fats, vitamins, and minerals are the fuel that the body needs to function properly. When you exercise, most of these substances are used up rapidly by the body and need replacement. When I ask individuals if they feel that their diet is correct in relation to the amount of activity they are involved in, their answer is frequently, "Yes, I get plenty of foods high in B vitamins, carbohydrates, proteins and fats." I have found that these individuals also monitor the nutritional values of foods and calculate their individual needs. Unfortunately, eating the proper amounts of foods and nutrients is only half the problem. A major concern of an athlete is that his or her system absorb and properly utilize the food ingested. Utilizing is the key word here because the food ingested usually lacks the proper enzymes. Enzymes are essential in the digestion of food and the release of nutrients into the body. Enzymes are present in the blood, muscles, tissues and organs and are involved in every metabolic function. Nothing can happen without enzymes. Nutrients cannot be used properly in the body, proteins cannot be digested and this can result in bloating, fatigue, stiffness, and hardening of the arteries. Undigested fats thicken the blood causing insufficient utilization of oxygen and cholesterol problems. The consequences of the lack of enzymes is innumerable but the point to recognize is that a missing link in good nutrition is enzymes.

A person who exercises regularly is concerned about getting and staying in shape. Strength and endurance are the goals of such individuals. How then can anyone achieve endurance if his blood cells are not getting the proper nutrients? Nutrients may be present in foods you eat, but the workforce of the body is in enzymes. This is why most vitamins are called co-enzymes. This means that they must combine with enzymes before the body can use them. Over-nutrition and under-absorption result in a low energy system. People often believe that they don't recover from exercise readily enough because they either overdid it or didn't do enough. The problem may actually be that the engine is congested with unusable fuel.

The more enzymes taken in orally through eating a good quantity of raw foods and supplementing your diet with enzymes, the more energy you will have. It has been said that half the amount of body energy is spent digesting food. If exogenous enzymes (enzymes taken through raw food or through supplementation) are added to the diet daily, more nutrients will be available and less food will be needed, resulting in less digestive stress and waste elimination. This is called energy conservation. The athlete will be able to work out more often and with greater intensity, and will require less recovery time.

Lou Piccone played ten years of professional football and was a driving force for the Buffalo Bills. He was the only player to master seven different positions on the team. When I met him, he weighed 210 pounds and stood 5'8" tall. By reducing his meat and dairy consumption and adding plant enzymes to his diet, he lost 30 pounds in two months. We trained together for a three-month period. His diet consisted of some fish and chicken but primarily fruits and vegetables. My diet consisted of fruits, vegetables, soaked seeds, nuts and rice. We both supplemented our diets with enzymes at each meal.

Lou then competed in the New York State Masters Track and Field events (also known as the Empire State Games) where he won five gold medals in his athletic events. Usually, when one loses thirty pounds by change of diet while in training, it is reported that one experiences a sense of weakness and a lack of energy. Lou's strength actually remained the same and his recovery time and endurance improved. Both Lou and I were entered in this competition during the summer of 1986 both at age 38. We ran in the 100- and 200-meter races and our finishing times were only a few tenths of a second short of our high school and college track times of almost twenty years ago.

When exercise or sport participation is considered, one must be healthy to carry out the program effectively. We must, out of necessity add to our enzyme reserve, not deplete it. It is great to enjoy sports and other related activities, but it will be a short-lived experience if our metabolic enzyme reserves are not maintained and we fail to supplement the daily losses to our system.

WHO SHOULD TAKE ENZYMES?

This is a question that only the individual can answer according to his own knowledge and understanding, but certain facts must be considered. Aging correlates perfectly with the enzyme reserve in the body. There is a greater amount of enzymes found in the young person's tissues than in an elderly person's tissues. Taking this into consideration, doing all you can to maintain and increase enzyme levels would be an advantage to tissue and organ longevity.

During all acute and chronic illnesses, enzymes are being used up more rapidly than is normal. If one is sick or trying to recover either from an acute or a chronic disease, taking enzyme supplements would be beneficial. People with hypoglycemia, endocrine gland deficiencies, obesity, anorexia nervosa, and stress-related problems, could all benefit from enzyme supplementation.

What about the athlete? He or she may be taking vitamins, minerals, and concentrated foods. What makes all of these elements work? Enzymes. Athletes can benefit by taking enzyme supplements because any time the body temperature is raised, as during exercise, enzymes are used up more rapidly than normal. Carbohydrates are burned faster, and more nutrients are needed for fuel supplies. The athlete usually eats mostly cooked food so it is like burning the candle at both ends. Enzymes are being used up rapidly and little is brought in to replenish the supply.

The human machine has an innumerable amount of enzymes. We will be hearing more and more about them in the future. As a person grows more health-conscious, he or she will certainly strive for a greater enjoyment of life. More energy, and a stronger mind and body will be needed to face the stresses that the future will bring. Enzymes can be instrumental in achieving such a goal.

The enzymes that the author is experienced with are manufactured by Foundation Enzyme, Wilmot, Wisconsin and distributed by Rainbow Light, Santa Cruz, California.

For Your Convenience On Cassette

FOOD ENZYMES:
The Missing Link to Radiant Health

by Humbart Santillo

Also included on these cassette tapes is information on:
• Enzymes as a foundation to health
• Enzymes and immunity
• Enzymes and weight loss

PLUS a copy of the book **FOOD ENZYMES: The Missing Link to Radiant Health** by Humbart Santillo $41.00 post paid

Send check or money order to:
Hohm Press, P.O. Box 2501, Prescott, Arizona 86302

ABOUT THE AUTHOR

Mr. Santillo was born and raised in Lockport, New York and received his B.S. degree from Edinboro State Teachers' College in Pennsylvania, attending on football and track scholarships.

Following graduation from Edinboro, Mr. Santillo developed thirty-three different allergies and signs of rheumatoid arthritis. After enduring three years of traditional medical treatment, and taking prescription drugs to no avail, Mr. Santillo began his search for a real solution to his problems. Over the course of many years he obtained the following degrees: Doctor of Naturopathy (Anglo-American Institute of Drugless Therapy), Health Practitioner (Hippocrates Health Institute of Boston, Mass. under Dr. Ann Wigmore and Victor Kulvinskas), Iridology Certificate of Merit (under Dr. Bernard Jensen), Master Herbalist (from Dr. John R. Christopher at the school of Natural Healing in Utah). Continuing his education, Mr. Santillo has attended many courses and seminars including: Oriental Herbal Medicine (with Sabhuti Dharmananda, Ph.D., Director of the Institute for Traditional Medicine and Preventative Health Care), Myopractic Therapy (with Dr. Jym Marinakas, N.D.), Medical Botany (from the Platonic Herbal Academy in Santa Cruz, California, with Ed Smith and Michael Tierra), and eight years of study under Dr. Phil Zimmerman and Dr. Thurman Fleet earning his Doctor's degree from the Concept-Therapy Institute, San Antonio, Texas.

NOTES

1. Chemical Reviews, 13: 501-12 (1933)
2. *Food Enzymes For Health & Longevity*, by Dr. Edward Howell — Introduction by Viktoras Kulvinskas, Pub. Omangod Press 1986
3. *Enzymes & Hormones* by Elizabeth D. McCarter, B.S., M.Ed. D.Sc. and Robert McCarter, B.S., M.S., Ph.D. Publishers — Bionomics Health Research Institute of Tucson 1983
4. See note 2 above.
5. Biochemistry Zeit, 208: 415-27 (1929)
6. Journal of Experimental Medicine, 55: 505-9 (1932)
7. Enzymologia, 1: 145-50 (1936)
8. Compt Rend. sociological biology, 112: 549-50 (1933)
9. Zeit, physiological chemistry, 221: 13-32 (1933)
10. Journal of clinical investigations, 13: 517-32 (1934)
11. American Journal of Digest. Dis. & Nut., 2: 230-5 (1935)
12. Proc Soc(iological) (Exp)periments (Bio)logy & (Med)icine, 28: 948-51 (1930-1)
13. *Enzyme Therapy*, Max Wolf, M.D. and Karl Ransbager, Ph.D. (Regent House, Los Angeles, CA, 1972)
14. Arch. F. Tierer v. Tierz. 4: 507-25 (1931)
15. Klin. Woch, 9: 2295-6 (1930)
16. Therap. Arch. U.S.S.R., 12: 140-4 (1934)
17. See note 2 above.
18. Sei-i-kai Mod. Journal, 54: 1531-8 (1935)
19. Arch. Verdanugskrankh, 49: 168-200 (1931)
20. Biochem. Zeit., 240: 328-56 (1931)
21. Amer. Journ. Digest. Dis., 5: 184-9 (1938)
22. Journal of Exptl. Zool., 76: 325-52 (1937)
23. *The McDougall Plan*, by John A. McDougall, M.D. & Mary A. McDougall (New Century Publishers, Inc., N.J., 1983)
24. Ziet, physiol. Chem. 221: 13-32 (1933)
25. Bibliotek for Larger, 123: 437-70 (1931)
26. Nagoya Journal of Medical Science 3: 51-73 (1928)
27. Biochem zeit. 275: 216-33 (1935)
28. "The Influence of Food Cooking on the Blood Formula of Man" by Paul Kouchakoff, M.D. (Institute of Clinical Chemistry, Lausanne, Switzerland, 1930)

29. *"Enzyme Nutrition"* by Dr. Edward Howell
30. Ibid.
31. Ibid.
32. Ibid.
33. Same as note 22 above.
34. Same as note 28 above.
35. Same as note 28 above.
36. *"Survival into the 21st Century"* by Viktoras Kulvinskas, (Omangod Press, Fairfield, Iowa, 1975)
37. Ibid.
38. Biochem. zeit. 288: 149-54 (1936)
39. Amer. Jour. Dig. Dis. & Nut. (Jan. 1934-5)
40. Same as note 2 above.
41. Journal of Nutrition, 13: 15-28 (1937)
42. Ibid., 12: 59-83 (1936)

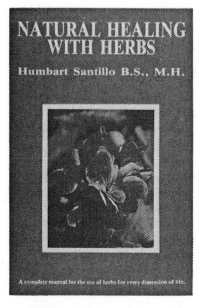

NATURAL HEALING WITH HERBS CORRESPONDENCE COURSE INFORMATION

This correspondence course has been written by the author for both the layperson and the physician. It is a course that will help prepare an individual to conduct his or her own herbal practice. The instruction presented in the course is unique in that it is coordinated with the material in the book, "Natural Healing With Herbs", which helps to make it simple for all to understand. Therapies utilizing nutritional foods, and both Chinese and American herbs (including their philosophies), are thoroughly discussed to furnish an understanding of both Eastern and Western medicine.

The course is divided into separate sections with questions and answers at the end of each section. Upon completion of the course, a final examination will be provided for the student to be completed and then mailed back to the author for correction. The student, upon satisfactorily completing the course, will receive his or her Master Herbalist Degree. There is no time schedule on completing the course; students may take six months, others one year. The student may proceed at his own pace.

The course is available for only $375.00 and an additional $16.25 if you have not purchased the book, "Natural Healing With Herbs". It is essential that the student purchase the entire course plus the book, "Natural Healing With Herbs" at the same time. (If two or more courses are ordered at the same time, you pay only $350.00 each.) If an individual prefers, he may make two payments. The first payment is $275.00 and includes only the first part of the course. A preliminary lesson preview is available for $7.00. The second part of the course will be mailed to the student upon receipt of the second payment of $100.00, which will be due within 30 days of the mailing date of the first part. (This includes shipping and handling charges.) A special price is offered to retail health food store owners or managers. Please write to the address below for more information. Make all checks or money orders (in U.S. funds only), payable to Humbart Santillo. Allow 3 - 4 weeks for delivery for courses paid by money order and 7 - 8 weeks for delivery for courses paid by check.

To assist the student, there are tapes available for purchase recorded live at herbal seminars given internationally by the author. They include further instruction of the proper use of herbs, diet, and the role the mind plays in healing.

Hundreds of people have been satisfied with this information. If within a two week trial period you find you are not satisfied with the material you have received, return the course for your refund minus $25.00 processing fee. This is a wonderful opportunity for the true seeker of herbal knowledge to receive proper, factual instruction.

To order courses or for more information, please write (no phone calls will be accepted): Herbal Correspondence Course, P.O. Box 468, East Amherst, New York, 14051.

HERBAL SEMINAR TAPES

These tapes are a live recording of an Herbal Seminar given to laymen, doctors, and other professionals by Mr. Santillo. The information begins with the basics of herbology and extends into a comprehensive coverage of therapies used in clinics throughout the world. It correlates historical herbology with the most recent in American and Chinese herbal philosophies. The tapes can be purchased with or without "Natural Healing with Herbs" Herbal Correspondence Course. Below is a description of the information available on each tape.

TAPE #1: Side A — This side explains the role that the mind plays in healing — how ideas and thoughts effect the body, and when negative, will result in dis-ease (disease). An interesting discussion is given explaining the parts of the brain and how they relay thought energy throughout the body, causing tension, stress, and other psychosomatic disorders. Once one understands this material, he or she is in a position to improve their mental attitude and avoid the negative effects of stress. The physical cause of disease is explained on this side along with other subjects such as acid-alkaline balance, cleansing diets, detoxification, enervation (lowered nerve energy), and toxemia. These subjects lead into a complete discussion on acute and chronic diseases and the difference between a healing crisis and a disease crisis. Then the dosages of herbs are discussed in the treatment of acute and chronic diseases.

Side B — The information here explains the three functions of herbs: eliminating, maintaining (balance), and building, and coordinating these with the healing properties of herbs, such as demulcents, laxatives, expectorants, etc. There are eight major therapies used to treat disease which are also discussed on this side, continuing to Tape #2, Side A.

TAPE #2:Side A — This tape explains therapies such as stimulation therapy, tranquilization therapy, blood purification and tonification therapies.

Side B — This side continues with more therapies such as sweating, emesis, diuresis, and purging. Herbs are listed under each therapy with a full discussion of what herbal properties are and their definitions.

TAPE #3:Side A — This tape gives a complete explanation of how to prepare and use herbal infusions, decoctions, boluses, douches, electuaries, pills, enemas, tinctures, and oils.

Side B — This side continues the discussion of the previous side with explanations of how to prepare and use poultices, plasters, castor oil packs (for the treatment of tumors), capsules, salves, and concentrates.

TAPE #4:Side A — In Chinese medicine, diseases are categorized as being either hot or cold. A discussion of this subject is presented along with suggested symptoms to look for help in determining illnesses of these two types. Dietary suggestions are given along with a cleansing diet and transition diet. Primary and secondary symptoms are discussed, along with how to determine one's major weaknesses and strengths. This gives the herbalist a basis to determine which part of the body to treat.

Side B — A thorough explanation is given on how to treat colds, fevers, and flus using cold sheet treatments, hydrotherapy, and the herbs fenugreek, catnip, fennel, comfrey, and thyme. Most important on this tape is an explanation of how to build proper herbal formulas for both acute and chronic illnesses. The final part of this side deals with how each disease goes through five stages of development from the onset to the cure. Symptoms are discussed so a therapist can recognize which stage the disease is in so that proper herbs can be chosen for that particular stage.

This is just an overview of some of the exciting subjects on these tapes. One can see how valuable this information is and also how difficult knowledge like this is to find. These tapes include concentrated, easy-to-understand information which can be of assistance to anyone who has the interest. These tapes are invaluable for laymen, doctors, or students who want to increase their own health or who want to help others.

Humbart D. Santillo, B.S., M.H.

The cost of this four-tape seminar, "Herbs, Nutrition, and Healing," is $41.00 post paid (U.S. funds only). Make checks payable to Hohm Press, P.O. Box 2501, Prescott, Arizona 86302.

Please send _____ copies of the book, *NATURAL HEALING WITH HERBS* at $16.25 post paid

Please send _____ copies of the tape series, *HERBS, NUTRITION AND HEALING* $41.00 post paid

Name _____

Address _____

City _____ State_____ Zip_____